BREAKING THE HIRING & TRAINING LOOP

BREAKING THE HIRING & TRAINING LOOP

MAYANK JAIN

Available on amazonkindle

Worldwide Published by

Pendown Press
PREMIUM BUSINESS PUBLISHER

PENDOWN PRESS LLP
An ISO 9001 & ISO 14001 Certified Co.,
Regd. Office: 3767A, Kanhaiya Nagar,
Tri Nagar, Delhi-110035
Ph.: 8130886000, 9650072927
E-mail: info@pendownpress.com
Branch Office: 1A/2A, 20, Hari Sadan, Ansari Road,
Daryaganj, New Delhi-110002
Ph.: 011-45794768
Website: PendownPress.com

Edition: 2025
Price: ₹ 399
ISBN: 978-93-6338-385-2

Layout and Cover Designed by Pendown Graphics Team
Printed and Bound in India by Thomson Press India Ltd.

To every small business owner who dreams big, works harder, and refuses to give up.

To those who wake up every day ready to build something better — even when the world doesn't notice.

This book is for you, with folded hands and deep respect.

May your journey be lighter, your dreams be brighter, and your growth be unstoppable.

Table of Contents

Preface

Business comes with countless challenges and opportunities. Among them, hiring, training, then hiring again and training again often become the biggest hurdles and can feel like an endless trap for most business owners.

That's why it needs your urgent attention right from the very start of your business journey.

Believe me, speaking from real experience, I have seen many people fail not because of a lack of product quality or business potential, but because they couldn't manage this one critical area effectively.

It's heartbreaking to watch talented entrepreneurs struggle simply because their team-building system was weak or reactive instead of proactive.

The good news is — **this major challenge can be addressed easily with small but powerful systematic strategies.** These strategies have already been tried, tested, and refined by countless successful business owners, and have consistently delivered outstanding results.

Implementing them from the beginning can save you time, money, and emotional energy, while setting a solid foundation for long-term success.

Acknowledgements

Whatever I have achieved in life, would have been impossible without the support of my parents. They've taught me unconditional love and I have seen them grow along with me. The wings that I have today would not have been possible without them.

To my wife, Divya, who has stood by me in every situation. You have handled all family responsibilities with great skill and dedication. Thank you from the bottom of my heart.

To my son, Taarush, who is the source of my happiness and inspiration. Lots of love!

My heartfelt gratitude to all my mentors and guides who have shown me light and direction in times of confusion.

To our clients, who have shared their experiences and knowledge with us during this journey. Thank you for trusting us and being our inspiration.

A special acknowledgement goes to Dinesh Verma and his exceptional team at Pendown Press. From the initial concept to the final manuscript, their support and expertise have made this book possible.

And finally, to all my loved ones who have been with me on this journey—thank you for your unwavering support, encouragement, and affection. Even if your names are not mentioned, you always hold a special place in my heart.

Without the support of all of you, it would not have been possible for me to move forward with confidence.

Author's Corner

Hi, I am Mayank Jain, a Chartered Accountant and Growth Specialist for SMBs.

I got my inclination towards outsourcing right from the time I started my career in 2011. I developed this inclination after seeing the powerful results it created across many industries. Those results grabbed my attention so much that I started using it for myself as well in the past.

But somewhere in the middle of my career, I started noticing a gap in the outsourcing model that needed to be fixed. The gap was to have a model where outsourcing could be offered as per the unique requirements of the business, that is, with a customized approach.

It's not easy to provide outsourcing on a customized basis, and therefore it was not readily available in the market. This gap hit me somewhere deep and I could clearly see this not just as a missing link but as a huge business opportunity for myself.

So after a few years of doing accounting stuff, I started approaching this model, seriously. I did a lot of studies, researched various methods, experimented, and applied them across multiple domains. This continuous juggle and exploration finally evolved into a model where we are now able to provide outsourcing services to business owners based on their specific requirements, with no fixed commitments and no exit barriers. That was truly a wow moment for me as well as for the industry, because it helped many businesses achieve their desired results faster and with much less risk.

We grew and helped many and many businesses in one way or another to come out of this invisible trap that can be really harmful for their business growth. Believe me, this is actually a trap, a cycle that becomes a loop and silently prevents growth in your business.

Later, with the time and experience, I realised that I could not be personally available to each and every business person to explain how this loop forms and how it can be broken very easily and effectively.

So I thought of penning down all my 15 years of experience related to this trap, the hard work I have put in, and the failures that I have faced in understanding it and finally reaching a stage where I was able to develop a few strategies that can actually help businesses come out of it.

This book also contains case studies and real-life examples of businesses from various industries which can be really relatable to each one of you, and can give you a clear context on how these strategies can be applied to your business practically.

I genuinely hope that the strategies shared in this book, along with live examples and case studies, will surely help many of us to come out of this trap and grow freely. These strategies are wonderful because they have already been tried, tested, and successfully implemented by many business owners, and have produced great results for them. So it is actually a no-brainer to implement them if you are serious about growth.

Please note this book is not meant only for reading but is meant for action-takers, for business owners who are stuck in this trap and are willing to come out of it. This can be achieved only by implementing these strategies actively in your business alongside reading.

So let's start with the content and see how it can be a mind-transformative journey for all of us.

Chapter - 1

Understanding the TRAP

The **Training Trap** is an invisible cycle that often leads businesses away from their core objectives, preventing them from achieving sustainable growth. Every business begins with a **clear vision**—whether it's to revolutionize an industry, create an exceptional product, or provide unmatched customer service. When a business owner starts out, they are deeply connected to their vision and make decisions in alignment with it. They can clearly see the mountain they want to climb and accordingly work with full energy to reach there.

But as the business grows, so do the challenges. The total workload on the owner becomes so much that it is practically impossible for one person to handle everything alone. And this is exactly where the TRAP starts. The business owner hires a team to help shoulder the responsibilities.

At this point, the **Training Trap** begins to take hold. The goal of hiring a team is to allow the owner to focus on the bigger picture—the ultimate vision. But what often happens is the exact opposite. The business owner gets occupied in an endless loop of **hiring, training, and rehiring** employees. Now, instead of progressing towards the ultimate vision, he is unknowingly diverted into working with an aim to just build and maintain a good team for the company.

Instead of freeing the owner to focus on growth, innovation, and strategic initiatives, they find themselves caught in a never-ending cycle of managing turnover. A survey by the **Society for Human Resource Management (SHRM)** reports that the average small business experiences **25-30% employee turnover** each year. This means a business might need to hire and train a quarter to a third of its workforce annually. This leads to significant losses—not just in time and energy but also directly affecting profitability and business momentum.

Over time, this invisible trap becomes one of the biggest hidden barriers to growth, silently draining the business of its potential without the owner even realizing it.

Case Study: Tech Startup - Rapidly Decreasing Profits Due to the Training Trap

Take the case of **TechCo (name changed)**, a fast-growing startup that specialized in software development. The company began with a small, tight-knit team of talented developers, all focused on the company's long-term vision: to create an innovative product that would disrupt the industry.

As TechCo began to scale, the founder realized the need for expanding her team. She needed help to meet the increasing demand and to focus more on long-term strategies.

She began hiring additional staff—developers, customer service representatives, and administrative assistants.

At first, it seemed like a good move.

The additional hands eased some burden.

But soon, the real issues began to surface.

Every time an employee left, whether due to personal reasons or a lack of alignment with the company's culture, the founder was forced to go through the tedious and **time-consuming process of hiring and training new employees.** This cycle became a major drain on both time and resources and critical resources.

TechCo's **profit margins started shrinking**, not just because of new salaries but due to the **high cost of continuous training and re-hiring**. After analyzing the impact, Sarah found that every time they had to replace a developer, the company lost nearly **50,000 in training and another 50,000 in downtime costs**, which together accounted for about 25% of their average annual revenue per employee.

The constant turnover and lack of stability meant that the company was never able to build the consistent momentum needed to achieve its core objectives. Instead of focusing on product development and scaling the business, the founder spent most of her time **in meetings, managing the onboarding process**, and worrying about the next employee who would inevitably leave.

TechCo's situation is a clear example of falling into the **Training Trap**. Instead of moving steadily towards the goal of smooth and strong scaling, the company was caught in a loop, continually putting out fires rather than building the future. As a result, profits stagnated, team morale dipped, and the company's core vision was left behind in the process.

The Cost of the Trap

This case is not unique. According to **Gallup**, SMBs that experience high turnover also experience **lower employee engagement, higher training costs**, and **significant losses in productivity**, all of which directly impact profitability. **The**

average cost of hiring and training a new employee can range between 33 to 50% of that employee's annual salary, depending on the industry. For a small business, this can be a crippling and recurring expense.

To avoid falling into the training trap, business owners must recognize the signs early on and take proactive steps to systematize their operations.

One of the smartest ways to do this is by leveraging outsourcing as a way to break free from the endless loop of hiring, retraining, and restarting.

Chapter - 2

The Myth of a Perfect Hire

As businesses grow, the temptation to rely heavily on the **"perfect hire"** becomes a common mistake. In the early stages, it's easy to believe that if you just hire the right person for each role, everything will fall into place. This belief often leads business owners to over-invest in hiring rather than focusing on building the systems that make those hires efficient and successful.

But here's the hard truth: **People alone cannot drive scalable growth.** While a dedicated and talented team can move things forward, it's **the systems** that make businesses capable of growing without friction, maintaining consistency, and staying adaptable to change.

The **"perfect hire"** is an illusion that many business owners chase. In the beginning, it seems like the right people—those who share your vision, possess all the right skills, and fit perfectly into your culture—can make everything run smoothly. However, this belief sets businesses up for disappointment and inefficiency.

Why?

Because even the most talented employee can't operate efficiently without a well-defined system to follow. And the truth is, **people are prone to human error**—they can get distracted, burn out, or face personal issues that impact their work. This dependency on perfect hires can create significant roadblocks when those employees leave or struggle to perform, causing delays and disruptions.

This gives a clear direction about the founder's real job:

It should be to develop scalable systems that the team can follow, rather than being dependent on individuals alone.

If you depend too much on people and ignore the systems, it eventually comes at a high cost to the business—both financially and strategically.

The Cost of Focusing on People Over Systems

Take the case of a small marketing agency that focuses solely on hiring talented marketers. At first, things went well because the owner has hired individuals who are experts in their field. However, as the business grows, the workload increases, and soon the business owner finds themselves **constantly hiring, training, and managing people**. The team members are talented, but they all have different working styles and methods. No one follows the same processes, resulting in **inconsistent deliverables**, missed deadlines, and frustrated clients.

Here are the problems that businesses face when relying on people over systems:

- **Inconsistent quality**: Without systems, employees may have different approaches to tasks, leading to varied quality and output.
- **Training burnout**: The constant need for training new employees can overwhelm the owner, taking them away from more important tasks.
- **Loss of momentum**: When employees leave, the business owner has to start from scratch, slowing down progress and delaying growth.

- **Dependence on individuals**: Relying on a few key employees or "rock stars" to carry the business can be dangerous if those people leave or underperform.

How System-Dependent Businesses Outgrow People-Dependent Ones

The businesses that succeed in the long term are those that **build and implement systems** that allow them to function smoothly, regardless of who is in charge. In system-dependent businesses, the core processes are standardized and automated as much as possible. Employees, whether new or experienced, are able to hit the ground running because the system provides clear guidance, reducing the need for constant training and micromanaging.

Systems ensure consistency, efficiency, and scalability. Whether it's customer support, sales, marketing, or product delivery, processes are well-documented, easy to follow, and adaptable to different situations. A **well-documented Standard Operating Procedure (SOP)** or automated workflow can replace hours of training and prevent costly mistakes.

Examples of Businesses That Escaped the Trap

Take the example of **SMB, an online** shoe retailer. When Zappos first began, it was a small operation with a team of customer service representatives doing everything manually. The founders soon realized that to scale their business, they couldn't just rely on hiring more people—they needed to create systems that would deliver a consistent, excellent customer experience without relying on every new hire to "figure it out."

By creating a **customer service system** that emphasized empowerment, training, and clear protocols, companies allowed their team to operate independently while maintaining high standards. The system didn't rely on individual performance, but rather, on a standardized approach that could be replicated across teams and locations. This foresight turned out to be the key to scaling rapidly, providing consistently high service without being trapped in the endless cycle of hiring and retraining.

Till now, we've explored what the **Training Trap** is and how people fall into it by believing in the **Myth of the Perfect Hire**. In the upcoming chapters, we'll discuss practical strategies and actions that can help you exit this trap and move toward more sustainable growth.

Chapter - 3

Employee Retention – Can This Take You Out from the Trap

Employee retention is often one of the most neglected yet critical systems in a growing business. Many founders fall into the trap of focusing only on hiring to fill gaps, often recruiting in a haphazard manner just to meet immediate needs without considering the long-term consequences. This is the first—and biggest—mistake a business owner can make. When employee retention is ignored from the very start, it slowly harms the foundation of the organization. Without a strong culture and a strategy to keep good employees, a company inevitably struggles with high turnover, reduced productivity, rising costs, and a disengaged workforce.

The Importance of Employee Retention

Employee retention is not just about keeping people around; it's about creating an environment where loyalty, trust, and commitment to the company's vision naturally grow. When people feel valued, they don't just stay—they contribute at a higher level.

According to a **Gallup study**, the **cost of replacing an employee** can range from **50% to 200% of that person's annual salary**, depending on the role. And this number only tells part of the story. The real cost includes lost knowledge, broken team momentum, lower morale, and sudden productivity dips that silently drain the business.

Many SMB owners, especially those leading blue-collar teams, often believe that employee retention strategies are not meant for them. They think that roles like warehouse workers, customer service reps, or factory staff don't need professional development, career growth, or deeper engagement.

THIS IS A BIG MYTH

This myth suggests that retention strategies and creating a culture of growth are only for white-collar, office-based businesses or industries. However, research proves otherwise. A study by the National Federation of Independent Business (NFIB) found that blue-collar workers who feel connected to their workplace culture and see opportunities for growth are far more likely to stay long-term and show higher levels of productivity.

Additionally, 70% of blue-collar workers in a recent survey indicated that they would stay longer at a company that invested in their growth and prioritized a positive work environment **(Source: Workplace Trends).**

In fact, focusing on retention strategies, even for blue-collar workers, can have a dramatic impact on a company's bottom line. Companies that **prioritize employee retention** report **20% lower turnover** and **15% higher customer satisfaction** (Gallup).

So all kinds of research whether for blue-collar or white-collar suggests that an EMPLOYEE RETENTION strategy is important in each and every scenario.

But wait—there's a contra view that often gets ignored. And interestingly, **it's backed by many studies too**.

Employee retention, if not handled properly, can make owners prone to blackmailing. Yes, that is right.

If business owners start believing that "retaining every employee at any cost" is the *only way* to escape the trap, they start making desperate efforts to hold on to people—sometimes at the cost of their own business health.

Here's how the trap unfolds:

As a business owner, handling appraisals and salary negotiations becomes one of the most uncomfortable things to do.

You don't want to give an unfair raise...

But you also don't want to demotivate your team or lose a good employee.

So, what happens?

You end up either:

1. **Giving in** to the demand, and then regretting it because it impacts your budget...
2. **Or saying 'no',** and feeling guilty for the next few months or leave them and get in the trap of training.

Here's the real problem:

Most business owners don't have a clear process of employee retention. They just "talk it out" in meetings, thinking that discussions will solve everything. But in the absence of a structured system, salary hikes and money start becoming the only retention tools left.

And once employees sense this... **blackmailing starts**—subtle at first, then direct.

In the next chapter, we'll talk about specific, actionable steps you can implement immediately to create strong employee retention without falling into emotional traps or financial blackholes.

Chapter - 4

The Building Blocks of an Employee Retention System

Creating a system for employee retention should not be an afterthought. It should start **the moment you hire your first employee**. Because once the foundation is strong, scaling becomes effortless:

1. **Understand Employee Needs: Money, Culture, and Growth**

   At the core of any successful retention strategy lie **three basic employee needs:**

   - **Money:** Competitive salaries are a given, today. But businesses that go a step further offering bonuses, health benefits, or even small financial perks, build stronger emotional loyalty. It's not just about *how much* you pay, but also *how thoughtfully* you structure it.
   - **Culture:** Every employee, whether on the shop floor or in a corporate office, wants to feel **valued and respected**. A positive, inclusive, and growth-focused company culture keeps employees emotionally invested far beyond the paycheck.
   - **Growth:** Employees stay when they **see a future** for themselves within your business. Opportunities for career advancement, training, new responsibilities, and personal development create that sense of future.

When these three pillars: Money, Culture, and Growth are addressed *systematically* from day one, **employees feel supported, motivated, and much more likely to stay**.

2. **Create a Clear Employee Journey from Entry to Exit**

   One of the most important elements of retention is the **employee journey**—the entire experience employees have from when they first join the company to when they leave (or ideally, retire). Mapping out this journey ensures that employees know what to expect and feel supported every step of the way. A well-defined journey helps employees see **how they can grow**, **what's expected of them**, and **how they'll be rewarded for their contributions**. Here's what a strong employee journey should look like:

   - **Entry:** From the moment an employee joins, they should have a clear understanding of their role, expectations, and the company culture.
   - **Development:** As employees grow within the company, offer **ongoing training**, **feedback sessions**, and opportunities to acquire new skills.
   - **Exit:** Whether it's a promotion, retirement, or resignation, design the exit experience in a way that employees leave feeling valued and respected.

   (Remember: *Ex-employees who leave on good terms often become your biggest brand ambassadors!*)

When employees feel that their journey is respected, their loyalty deepens.

3. **Onboarding as the First Step**

   A **structured onboarding process** is one of the simplest but most impactful retention strategies. Onboarding should not just be about filling out forms and explaining company policies; it should set the tone for the employee's entire journey within the company.

A few key elements of a great onboarding process include:

- **Welcome presentations:** Go beyond job descriptions. Share your company's *mission*, *vision*, and *dreams*. Make new hires feel like they are part of something bigger than just a job.
- **Company culture immersion:** Introduce them to the *way things are done here*. Let them feel the spirit, energy, and values of your workplace, right from the start.
- **Training and professional development:** Provide them with the tools and training needed to succeed in their role and progress within the company.

According to research by Glassdoor, employees are **58% more likely** to stay at a company for **three years or more** if they have a positive onboarding experience

4. **Continuously Assess Employee Satisfaction and Engagement**

   Retention doesn't happen by accident—it requires constant care and attention. Founders must regularly **check in with employees to** assess job satisfaction and engagement. Don't assume things are fine just because no one is complaining. Use tools like employee surveys, feedback loops, and regular one-on-one meetings to ensure employees feel heard and supported.

5. **Employee Growth Framework**

   A strong growth framework includes two essentials:

1. **Clear Career Pathways:** Define progression paths for employees to help them understand how they can grow within the company, making long-term retention more likely.
2. **Ongoing Learning & Development:** Offer continuous training, workshops, and learning opportunities to help employees expand their skill sets and advance in their roles.

6. **Feedback System**

   Having a strong **feedback system** with employees is **not just important; it's essential**.

   It gives people a deep, powerful feeling: *"I am being asked. I am being heard."*

   And this feeling matters **more today than ever before**.

   The purpose of employment has **evolved** significantly over the last 100 years:

   - **100 years ago**: People worked simply to **earn a livelihood**, to meet basic needs like food and shelter.
   - **Later generations**: Work became a way to **improve the standard of living**; buying homes, cars, and comforts.
   - **Today**: The purpose of work has shifted again.

   People now seek **quality of life with work**; they want respect, growth, fulfillment, and a workplace where their voice matters.

In this new world, a feedback system is not just a management tool; it's a **bridge to human connection**.

When you have regular feedback mechanisms, you fulfill one of the deepest needs of modern employees:

To be heard. To feel valued. To be seen.

7. **Employee Engagement**

1. **Open Communication:** Foster a culture of transparency and openness where employees feel safe to share their ideas, feedback, and concerns. When employees know they can speak up without fear, it builds **deep trust and loyalty**.
2. **Recognition & Empowerment:** Regularly recognize and celebrate employees' efforts, big or small. Give them **autonomy** in their decision-making wherever possible. When employees feel **trusted and appreciated**, they bring their best selves to work every single day..

> *"Recognition isn't a bonus—it's a basic human need."*

Conclusion: Building a Retention System That Works

The key to long-term business success lies in creating an employee retention system that is **proactive**, not reactive. Business owners need to shift their focus from just **filling positions** to **building systems** that cater to the **needs** of their workforce. Whether your team is composed of white-collar professionals or blue-collar employees, prioritizing **money, culture, and growth** is the **cornerstone** of an effective retention strategy.

By creating an environment where employees feel **valued**, have **clear career paths**, and experience **support at every stage**, from entry to exit; you unlock powerful results:

- **Lower turnover**
- **Higher morale**
- **Better productivity**
- **Stronger profitability**

Remember:

"Companies don't grow because of ideas alone. They grow because of the people who believe in those ideas and stay to build them."

Chapter - 5

ABC of Making Your Company System-Dependent (Releasing Dependency from Employees)

Research and industry studies consistently show that for businesses to scale effectively and stay on track with their goals, they must shift from being **employee-dependent** to being **system-dependent**.

Having systems in place allows the business to function smoothly without relying on the whims or availability of individual employees. This transformation is crucial for sustainable growth and ensuring that the vision of the company is met consistently. So, how can we start making this shift?

The first step is to **list all the processes** in your business that are currently **employee-dependent**, especially those where you face constant issues like **blackmailing, delays, or work bottlenecks**. These are the areas that require urgent attention. Identifying these pain points will help you prioritize which processes need to be systematized first to minimize dependency on any one individual.

Now, let's address a common myth that many founders believe: **"My employees are too experienced and loyal to be replaced. They know the processes, and I don't, so I'm stuck relying on them."**

Here's why this myth can harm your business:

- **Research by McKinsey** has shown that businesses that depend heavily on individual employees (even experienced ones) for key processes **are at greater risk** when those employees leave or are unavailable. **Even the most experienced employees have knowledge gaps** that can create vulnerabilities in the business.
- A **Harvard Business Review** article on "Building a System-Dependent Company" emphasizes that **systems**, not individuals, ensure continuity. Once systems are put in place, businesses can smoothly transition, even if long-term employees leave or retire.

The truth is, **systemizing processes** allows you to reduce this dependency and helps future-proof your business. By documenting processes and implementing systems, you create a framework that can work efficiently without relying on any one person—regardless of their tenure with the company. Having strong systems does not reduce the importance of having a good team. It enhances it.

This focus on building a system-dependent company is not about undervaluing employees; rather, it is a professional strategy that prepares your business for scaling up, making it immune to blackmailing threats, sudden employee exits, or operational disruptions.

It is a necessary step towards building a resilient organization where the vision, culture, and performance are not tied to any one person, but flow smoothly through **well-documented, clear processes**.

Chapter - 6

Starting with Training Module

Once you've identified the processes that need special attention, the next crucial step is to **develop a proper, defined, and labeled training module**. This is where the real work begins. Without a structured training framework, even the best systems can break down, so it's essential to document everything meticulously. A training module is not just about instructions; it's about creating a process that everyone can follow consistently.

The first action is to **list out all activities** within each process that need to be carried out. Every single step in a process must be documented and should contain detailed information on:

- **How to execute each step**: This includes the **method** or procedure for performing the task.
- **Documents required**: All forms, templates, or resources necessary for the task.
- **Communication guidelines**: What needs to be communicated during each step, both **internally** (to your team) and **externally** (to clients or customers). Also, note the communication that should happen **after the task is completed**. Clear communication bridges gaps and fosters better teamwork.

Additionally, **problem-solving mechanisms** should be built into the process documentation. You need to define how to address any common blockages or issues that could arise. Problems are inevitable, but being prepared for them creates a smoother workflow. If something new pops up, the document should specify **who to contact** and how to escalate the issue. This ensures that no step gets stuck, and everyone knows how to troubleshoot in real-time, reducing unnecessary delays.

Let's take an example to understand how this module can be framed to start with and what all steps should be involved in drafting it:

I am taking a generic process example here so that most of us can relate to it. Let's take a part of the **accounting process** as an example. Here's how you'd break it down:

1. **Step 1: Invoice Receipt**
    - **How to do it**: The first step is receiving and logging the invoices. This should be done by the accounts assistant. Ensure that the invoice is verified for accuracy and logged promptly in the system.
    - **Documents Required**: Invoice template, purchase order, and receipts.
    - **Communication**: Notify the procurement team about the received invoice and check if the details align with the purchase order.
    - **Problem Solving**: If the invoice doesn't match the purchase order, it should be flagged for review. Contact the procurement manager for clarification.
2. **Step 2: Invoice Processing**
    - **How to do it**: Process the invoice for payment. This includes entering the details into the accounting software.

- **Documents Required**: Invoice number, date, amount, and vendor details.
- **Communication**: Send a confirmation email to the vendor about the payment timeline.
- **Problem Solving**: If there's a delay in processing, contact the senior accountant to approve the delay and reschedule the payment. Notify the vendor of any changes to the timeline.

3. **Step 3: Payment Approval and Execution**
   - **How to do it**: Once processed, the payment request needs senior management's approval. Ensure the proper checks are in place before proceeding to payment.
   - **Documents Required**: Payment request form, invoice copy, vendor details.
   - **Communication**: Notify the finance manager for final approval.
   - **Problem Solving**: If the payment is delayed, escalate to the CEO for immediate approval.

And SO ON ...

By documenting each step, you ensure that every person who handles the accounting process knows exactly what to do and when:

When every step in the accounting process is documented, it creates a **clear structure** for the entire team to follow. This eliminates subjectivity and confusion. Whether it's a new hire or an existing employee, they'll have a set path to follow, ensuring consistency and reducing errors. The key takeaway is: **clarity**. New hires can be quickly onboarded with the **Standard Operating**

Procedures (SOPs), and current employees are always guided by a predefined process.

Personal Touch - A Common Concern:

People have always believed in the power of **eye-to-eye contact**. They feel that some things are better explained in person than through written documentation. **The question arises:** Should we go back to the old-school methods of training—spending a significant amount of time giving in-person training to every new hire? Or is there a way to modernize the process without compromising quality?

This is a valid concern, and the reality is that **traditional training models** can be resource-intensive and time-consuming, especially when scaling a business. But here's the good news: **There's always a solution if we approach it strategically.**

Strategic Solution: Develop Training Videos for Key Processes

To overcome the challenges of traditional training, we need to **blend the best of both worlds**—maintaining personal interaction while using modern tools for efficiency. **Video training** is the perfect bridge.

Creating training videos allows you to:

- **Reduce time spent on training by up to 90%.**
- **Allow employees to learn at their own pace** without feeling the pressure of in-person training.
- **Reduce redundancy** in training efforts as employees can revisit videos whenever needed.

This looks easy to start off with but when making my clients do this, I have faced some of their fears and myths. I am discussing a few most common myths which I have come across in recent times.

1. **Many business owners think that documenting processes and creating training modules is time-consuming and unnecessary. They believe that their team can "figure it out" as they go.**

   Here's the truth: Without a clear and documented system, tasks are bound to get lost in translation, leading to inefficiencies, errors, and frustrations.

2. **"My team already knows the process, so why document it?"**

   - **Truth**: Studies show that companies with documented systems and processes see 30% higher efficiency in day-to-day operations. Employees are more likely to follow a process when it's laid out clearly. And as team members change or grow, documentation ensures continuity.
   - **Source**: **Institute of Management Accountants (IMA)** reports that **82% of successful companies** attribute their efficiency to having well-documented processes.

3. **"We don't have time to create detailed training modules."**

   - **Truth**: While creating systems may feel like a heavy lift, it saves significant time and money in the long run. A **Deloitte study** revealed that **companies with formalized training programs** saw a **40% increase in retention** and a **24% increase in productivity.** This in turn gives companies a good increase in profit directly without working on sales and marketing.

Conclusion

The key to building a business that runs smoothly without over-relying on employees is documenting everything–**step-by-step**. It's about creating a foundation that works, whether the team members stay or go. By starting with the right training modules and addressing all areas of your business through defined processes, you set the stage for long-term success. A company needs to invest some of its time and money to develop a world-class training module with the help of professional companies who specialize in this area. This is a one-time great investment which, if done properly and timely, will produce great results in the long run.

No more chaos. No more bottlenecks. Just clear, repeatable systems that work every time. Make that investment today, and watch your business thrive tomorrow.

Chapter - 7

Training Videos and Personal Touch

When it comes to training, having a clear, documented **training module** is just the beginning. While the process guidelines and reporting structures are essential, there's something equally important—**your personal body language during** the training. It's not just about what you say, but **how you say it**.

Your passion, energy, and the way you communicate your vision **speak volumes** about your company, and this impacts how the new hires perceive their role and the organization's direction.

But how do you convey that "personal touch" without getting caught in endless one-on-one training sessions? How do you make sure new employees understand your vision, company structure, and HR policies without spending days repeating the same information?

This is where training videos come in.

Repetitive Information and Time-Saving

There's a lot of information that every new hire needs to know—**the company vision, organizational structure, HR policies**, and expectations. This is crucial for aligning them with your culture and values. But when **high attrition rates are** involved, business owners spend far too much time repeating the same things over and over.

It's not just about **administrative stuff** either. Technical aspects of the job, such as for **sales** roles, can be highly repetitive. Information like:

- Product knowledge
- Market insights
- CRM system usage
- Reporting structure
- Incentives and targets

...these remain the same every time a new person comes on board. In fact, they usually cover about **80%** of the training content. So, what's the solution to reduce this burden?

Saving Time and Efforts Through Training videos

Instead of wasting time on **repetitive explanations**, businesses are now using **training videos** to cover the basics. Here's how it works:

1. **Pre-recorded Videos**: These videos can explain things like:
    - The company's mission and vision
    - HR policies and employee benefits
    - Organizational structure
    - General expectations

Once the new employee watches these videos, HR can hold a **live session** to address any questions or clarifications they might have. This way, they get the standard orientation without taking up hours of the business owner's time.

2. **Role-Specific Training Videos**: For technical roles, like sales, you can create videos detailing:
   - Product offerings
   - CRM system navigation
   - Sales targets and how to report
   - Incentives structure

Once these initial videos are consumed, the employee can then have a **one-on-one session** with a technical expert to solve any lingering doubts.

Many businesses at times feel that their employees won't learn effectively from videos, fearing that they won't feel as engaged or connected compared to face-to-face explanations. This is a common concern, but the truth is, training videos can be just as impactful—if not more so—than traditional methods.

Why? Because:

- **Engagement**: Training videos can be more engaging, especially when they're dynamic, using visuals and real-life examples to keep employees interested.
- **Pace Control**: Employees can learn at their own pace. They can pause, rewind, or fast-forward to key sections, which allows them to absorb information without the pressure of keeping up with a live trainer.
- **Consistency**: Videos ensure every employee receives the exact same training content, minimizing any inconsistencies that may arise in one-on-one training sessions.
- **On-Demand Access**: Employees can revisit the training videos whenever they need a refresher. This makes them feel more confident as they can rely on these resources whenever they encounter challenges in their roles.

Research Backing the Effectiveness of Video Training

Research from **LinkedIn Learning** found that **58% of employees prefer to learn at their own pace**, with many opting for video-based training because it allows them to review content as needed. Furthermore, **a study by the Brandon Hall Group** revealed that **companies using video-based training see a 34% increase in employee retention** and a **29% improvement in learning application** compared to those relying solely on in-person training.

Employees are perfectly capable of learning effectively from videos—especially if the content is well-structured, concise, and relatable. Moreover, videos can be revisited anytime, which ensures better retention and understanding. The myth that employees need in-person training to absorb information is simply outdated.

The Key: Structure, Not Capability

The reason why it doesn't work is not employees and their capabilities, it's about structure and the science businesses follow to make these kinds of modules and videos. If the structure is not right, it will certainly defeat the purpose.

As a result of my constant interaction with the businesses, I have found that owners feel that they need to track whether each employee has properly watched the videos and understood them. If they haven't, it could directly impact the business results, and owners don't want to take that chance.

Do you also feel the same pain? Is this a major reason why we should spend so much of our time in this trap?

Is this the right reason for deviating from our goal and vision?

The answer has to be NO.

We are in an era of technological advancement and AI. There are lots of software and tools in the market that are capable enough to ensure that the videos given are properly watched and understood. These tools can track the speed at which videos are watched, restrict fast-forwarding, limit skipping to the next video, and automatically generate questions to check comprehension—giving you real-time tracking.

So, again, it's not about the employees or the system preventing businesses from using video training. It's about having the right structure and expertise to create a self-working mechanism and free you from the trap in your business.

Why This Works

The beauty of this system is that it reduces the **burden on the business owner** while still providing the **personal touch that** every new employee needs. You don't have to spend hours repeating basic information. Instead, you can focus on delivering more **contextual, role-specific training** and answering the **questions** that matter most. This shift not only frees up your time but also ensures that your employees have a **clear understanding** of both the company's goals and their role in it.

In short, **training videos** give you the best of both worlds: **efficiency and effectiveness**. You get to deliver crucial information without losing your time, while also adding a personal touch during follow-up sessions.

Case Study: A Business Owner's Experience

Let's look at the result of one of my Noida-based client, a small but growing tech company. Before they adopted the video-based training model, the founder was spending an average of **7 full days** onboarding each new employee. This meant they were not only taking time away from critical tasks, but also facing delays in productivity. After implementing a training video system, new employees were up to speed in just **3 days** with only **1-2 hours** of involvement from a senior team member. This not only **cut down training time by over 50%**, but also saved the company significant money by reducing the need for constant management involvement in the process.

Conclusion

Using training videos doesn't just make your training process faster and more efficient—it also helps your business scale without losing that all-important **personal connection**. Employees appreciate the clarity of a well-structured training system, and you'll appreciate the time and money saved. This approach will help you onboard employees quickly, reduce attrition, and maintain consistent quality across your team.

By moving beyond the traditional "one-size-fits-all" training sessions and embracing **video-based learning**, you're setting your company up for smoother, faster, and more scalable growth.

Chapter - 8

The Easiest Option - OUTSOURCING (THE HACK)

As a business owner, the options for scaling and improving your business systems may seem daunting. The complexity of setting up **training modules**, **employee retention systems**, or transitioning to a **system-dependent** business might look overwhelming. Often, these solutions require **personal involvement** from the founder, especially in the initial stages. This can create a bottleneck, where business owners find it difficult to take **decisive action** because they simply **lack the time** or expertise to implement these changes.

This is where **outsourcing** becomes the game-changer. Outsourcing is often viewed as the quickest and most effective way to overcome resource limitations and gain the support needed to **keep operations running smoothly**. By outsourcing non-core functions, businesses can focus on what they do best while leveraging external expertise to handle the rest.

What is Outsourcing?

At its core, outsourcing means **handing over responsibility for specific processes** or functions within your business to a **trusted third-party partner**. This partner can manage everything from **process management** to **resources**, and you, as the business owner, are left to focus on higher-level objectives, **strategic planning**, and **growth**.

This approach allows you to **delegate** the operational complexity without sacrificing control over the outcomes. You can track the results of the outsourced process, but you don't have to get bogged down in the day-to-day details.

The Power of Outsourcing: Real-Life Example

Let's take the **HR process** as an example. The HR function in a growing business often becomes a significant drain on time and resources. From **recruiting, onboarding, employee training**, to **managing benefits** and **compliance**, HR involves a complex set of tasks that demand specialized knowledge and attention.

Instead of hiring an in-house HR team, you can **outsource** the entire HR function to an experienced agency or service provider. The outsourcing partner will handle everything from **candidate sourcing, interviews, employee benefits, payroll**, and even **performance management**, while you remain in control of the **final outcomes**—such as **employee satisfaction, retention rates**, and **organizational performance**.

For example, you could hire an HR outsourcing agency like **XYZ HR Solutions**, who will handle all the technicalities, leaving you to simply review reports and track metrics that align with your business goals. This allows you to **free up your time** and avoid the distraction of managing every single detail.

Why Outsourcing Is The Easiest Option

Outsourcing offers several distinct advantages, especially for startup founders and small business owners who need to **focus on scaling:**

1. **Immediate Expertise**: When you outsource, you tap into the **knowledge** and **experience** of a specialized team who already know how to execute a particular process effectively. There's no need to go through a lengthy trial-and-error phase.
2. **Resource Efficiency**: By outsourcing, you save on the costs associated with recruiting, training, and retaining full-time employees for tasks that don't require your direct attention. Instead of hiring in-house staff for each function, you only pay for the services you need, as they are needed.
3. **Scalability**: Outsourcing allows your business to **scale** quickly without being limited by internal resource constraints. You don't need to constantly worry about **hiring more people** or adding more tasks to your plate because a trusted outsourcing partner handles those processes.
4. **Focus on What Matters Most**: By offloading complex processes to external partners, you regain the time and energy to focus on what really matters—**growing the business**, improving your product or service, and **building strong customer relationships**.

Outsourcing simplifies the complexities of business operations, giving you the space to lead your company to new heights while ensuring that essential tasks are in expert hands.

The Myth: Outsourcing Means Losing Control

A common myth about outsourcing is that it means you lose **control** over the processes and results. However, the reality is that **outsourcing gives you control in a different way**. Rather than being overwhelmed by micromanaging every aspect of a process, you **track results** and monitor performance metrics. You set the **expectations**, and the outsourcing partner takes responsibility for meeting those expectations. It's not about losing control; it's about **gaining strategic control** over your time and resources.

In fact, the **success of outsourcing** lies in clear communication, **well-defined goals**, and **regular performance reviews**. When done correctly, outsourcing doesn't remove your control—it simply shifts the focus to **higher-level management** while the day-to-day operations are handled efficiently by external experts.

Conclusion

Outsourcing is often the simplest solution when it comes to **freeing up your time** and tackling tasks that require specialized knowledge. Whether it's managing your **HR function**, **marketing**, or **customer service**, outsourcing allows you to delegate without worrying about the details. By **outsourcing effectively**, you not only relieve yourself of operational burdens but also ensure that your business is aligned with the expertise and resources needed to thrive.

When the task seems too big or tough to handle in-house, **outsourcing is your shortcut to scaling up without the growing pains.** It's not about avoiding work, but rather about being strategic in how you allocate resources. If done right, outsourcing can become one of your greatest allies in driving scalable, sustainable growth for your business.

Chapter - 9

The How of Outsourcing

The Breakthrough Hack to Escape the Training Trap

It's time for a revelation–a **hack** that not only frees you from the **never-ending cycle of hiring, training, and retraining** but also **drives real, measurable results** for your business. As discussed in Chapter 8, **outsourcing is not just a convenience—it's a strategy** that successful businesses use to **scale, cut costs, and focus on their core objectives**.

However, **outsourcing without a plan** is like hiring without a job description–you won't get the results you expect. Many business owners **start with a poor outsourcing strategy**, face challenges, and then **dismiss outsourcing as ineffective**, when in reality, **they just didn't implement it correctly**.

The key to **successful outsourcing** is **starting with a well-defined strategy**. Here's how to **structure and execute outsourcing in a way that drives maximum impact**.

Step 1: Identify Your Business Processes

The first step is to **list all the processes in your business**. Imagine your company as a machine, each part working together to ensure smooth operations. Some of these processes directly contribute to revenue generation, while others, although crucial for day-to-day operations, may not have a direct link to business growth.

Categorization of Business Processes:

Once you have listed them, divide them into four major categories:

- **Primary Processes:** These are the core activities that drive revenue and growth, such as sales, product development, and marketing efforts.
- **Back Office Processes:** These functions, while essential to keep the business running smoothly, are non-customer-facing. Examples include data entry, HR management, and accounting..
- **Accounting Processes:** Financial operations such as payroll, invoicing, and bookkeeping fall into this category.
- **Support Processes:** Customer service, IT support, sales support and admin tasks.

Step 2: The 5-Point Process for Outsourcing

Once categorized, you can further **segment** the processes based on the **action required**:

1. **Eliminate**: Remove redundant tasks that no longer serve a purpose (e.g., outdated reporting, manual work replaced by automation).
2. **Outsource**: Identify **highly repetitive processes** that can be handed over to an outsourcing partner. This includes tasks like **customer support, data entry, HR administration, and IT management**.

3. **Delegate**: Certain **one-time or non-recurring** tasks (such as website design or content writing) can be handled by freelancers or temporary project-based teams.
4. **Create** – Some **missing processes** may emerge that need to be built from scratch. These could include **automation workflows, CRM integrations, or internal training programs**.
5. **Do It Yourself** – Some critical, high-value processes **must stay in-house** (e.g., business strategy, key client relationships).

This classification ensures that you **don't outsource everything blindly** but rather **follow a structured approach** to streamline operations efficiently.

Step 3: Start Small – Outsource Support Processes First

For business owners new to outsourcing, the best way to **gain confidence** in the process is to **start with small, low-risk functions** before transitioning to more critical areas.

Example: Outsourcing Customer Support & Back Office Operations

Many startups initially **struggle with customer support**, often leading to **missed inquiries, delayed responses, and ultimately, poor customer experience**. Outsourcing **customer service and back-office operations** to a professional agency can provide immediate relief and deliver several key benefits:

- **Efficiency:** Calls, emails, and chats are handled promptly, ensuring no customer query goes unanswered.
- **Customer Satisfaction:** Faster response times result in higher levels of customer satisfaction and loyalty.
- **Time Savings:** The business owner can save 10-15 hours per week, freeing up time to focus on high-priority tasks, like strategic planning and business growth.

A case study by **Deloitte** found that **businesses that outsourced customer support saw a 33% reduction in customer churn** and a **40% increase in overall efficiency**.

By starting with non-core processes like **customer support, data entry, or payroll management**, you get **quick wins** that help you trust the outsourcing model before scaling it to other areas. These initial successes will help build your confidence and make it easier to scale outsourcing to other areas of your business as you grow.

Step 4: Set Up a Clear Monitoring & Tracking System

One of the biggest myths surrounding outsourcing is **"If I outsource, I lose control."** In reality, **businesses that outsource successfully actually gain more control**—because they set up **tracking mechanisms** that give them real-time insights into their processes.

How to Ensure Control Over Outsourced Processes:

- Use **CRM & Ticketing Systems** to track customer support efficiency.

- Set **Key Performance Indicators (KPIs)** to measure performance (e.g., resolution time, customer satisfaction).
- Have **weekly or monthly reports** from your outsourcing partner to review progress.
- Regularly **audit** outsourced processes to ensure **alignment with business goals.**

A study by **McKinsey & Co.** shows that **companies that establish clear KPIs for their outsourcing partners see a 25-30% improvement in operational efficiency** compared to those that don't.

Conclusion: How to Get Started with Outsourcing Today

Let's review: Outsourcing is not about **losing control** or **handing over your business to someone else**–it's about **freeing yourself from operational burdens** and **focusing on high-value growth activities**.

By following this structured approach:

- Identifying and categorizing your business processes
- Eliminating redundant tasks
- Outsourcing repeatable processes
- Delegating project-based tasks
- Monitoring performance through tracking systems

You create a **scalable, efficient, and system-driven business** that is **not dependent on you or your employees** for day-to-day operations.

The **biggest mistake** business owners make is **waiting too long to outsource**–by the time they realize they need it, they are already buried under inefficiencies and it becomes harder to break free. The sooner you **start with small steps**, the faster you can **break free from the training trap** and focus on **scaling with confidence**.

Remember, outsourcing isn't a one-time fix—it's an ongoing strategy that will evolve as your business grows. Start now, and you'll build the foundation for success that lasts.

Chapter - 10

Outsourcing in the STARTUP ERA

We've reached the final step for outsourcing, where it's time to think and formulate a strategy that works for your business. However, at this stage, **many business owners still hesitate to take the final leap—outsourcing**.

Why? Because of one BIG myth:

"Outsourcing is only for big companies; small businesses can't afford it."

Outsourcing is NOT Just for Large Enterprises

This is the **biggest lie** that holds back SMBs from scaling efficiently. Let's break it down with some **real facts**:

66% of small businesses outsource at least one function to stay lean and focus on growth (Statista, 2024).

Deloitte's Global Outsourcing Report found that SMBs that outsource **save 30-50% in operational costs**, allowing them to reinvest in their core business.

A study by Clutch.co reported that SMBs outsourcing customer support, accounting, and admin work saw a **40% improvement**

in operational efficiency within the first year.

Still not convinced? Let's look at real-world examples:

Case Study 1: The Startup That Scaled from 3 to 50 Employees Without an HR Team

A SaaS startup, originally with **just three employees,** was struggling to manage recruitment, payroll, and compliance. Hiring an in-house HR team was **too expensive**, so they **outsourced HR management to a specialized agency**.

- Within **6 months**, they onboarded **50+ employees** smoothly.
- Employee **retention increased by 35%,** thanks to improved hiring processes and better onboarding practices.
- The founders saved **10+ hours per week**, allowing them to **focus on scaling the business**.

Case Study 2: The Small E-commerce Brand That Outsourced Customer Support

A small e-commerce business selling fashion accessories was losing customers due to **slow response times and inconsistent support**. Hiring a full-time team was **too costly**, so they outsourced customer service to a professional agency.

- Response time **dropped from 24 hours to under 2 hours**.
- Customer satisfaction **increased by 50%**, leading to more repeat purchases.
- With more time on their hands, the owner focused on ***marketing and product expansion***, ultimately doubling revenue within a year.

How to Implement Outsourcing Without Losing Control

One of the biggest fears business owners have is, **"If I outsource, I'll lose control over my operations."** But **outsourcing does not mean handing over your business to someone else—it means freeing yourself from repetitive tasks while still maintaining oversight**.

Here's how you **outsource without losing control**:

1. **Start Small:** Begin by outsourcing just **one process**, like customer support, admin work, or payroll.
2. **Set Clear Expectations:** Define **KPIs (Key Performance Indicators)** so you can measure success and keep everything on track.
3. **Use Monitoring Tools:** CRM systems, dashboards, and regular reports provide real-time insights into performance and progress.
4. **Have a Feedback Loop:** Conduct weekly or monthly reviews with your outsourcing partner to ensure alignment with your goals and make necessary adjustments.

The Final Takeaway: Why SMBs Should Outsource NOW

Many small business owners wait too long to outsource, and by the time they realize they need help, they're already bogged down with problems and can't grow. If you're spending **too much time managing employees, fixing errors, and handling admin work**, it's time to **stop working IN your business and start working ON your business**.

- Outsourcing lets you focus on strategy and growth.
- It reduces operational costs and improves efficiency.
- It makes your company system-dependent, not people-dependent.

The question is not whether outsourcing works. The question is—how long will you wait before making it work for YOU?

Conclusion: Breaking Free from the Training Trap

"The definition of insanity is doing the same thing over and over again and expecting different results."

— Albert Einstein

As we come to the end of this book, one thing should be crystal clear: the Training Trap is real, and it is silently stealing your time, money, and business growth. If left unaddressed, it keeps you trapped in a never-ending cycle of hiring, training, rehiring, and retraining—keeping you distracted from your real goal: scaling your business and bringing your original vision to life.

But here's the good news—there is a way out. The chapters you've read provide a detailed blueprint to break free from this cycle. The most important step now is to take action.

A Customized Approach: The Right Mix for Your Business

There is no one-size-fits-all approach to breaking the Training Trap. Each business has different needs, time constraints, and resource availability. That's why you don't have to implement all strategies at once. Instead, take a phased approach that suits your situation:

1. **Start by acknowledging the problem:** Understand that being stuck in this cycle is taking you away from your core goals. If you don't take action, nothing will change. Awareness is the first step to transformation.
2. **Analyze your business processes:** Identify the areas that are eating up most of your time—whether it's constant hiring, inefficient training, or lack of systemization.
3. **Choose a strategic mix:** Depending on your time and availability, you can pick a balanced approach:
    - ➢ **If you have time:** Focus on building a structured training module and set up a system-dependent company where employees work within clearly defined processes.
    - ➢ **If you are overwhelmed:** Consider outsourcing repetitive tasks so you can focus on core business functions.
    - ➢ **If you are somewhere in between:** A mix of structured hiring, training, and outsourcing can help you optimize your operations while ensuring quality control.

"You do not rise to the level of your goals. You fall to the level of your systems." — James Clear, Atomic Habits

The companies that scale fast are not the ones who hire the best employees, but the ones who create the best systems.

The Breakthrough Mindset:
Escaping the Comfort Zone

Many business owners are trapped by the false belief that the only way to scale is by hiring and training more employees. But history has shown that this isn't always the case:

- **McDonald's** did not become a global giant because of great chefs—it became a system-dependent business where anyone could follow a process and deliver the same results.
- **Amazon** didn't grow due to excellent warehouse workers; it exploded because of well-defined logistics and automated fulfillment systems that allowed them to handle massive scale with minimal human intervention.
- **A small e-commerce company** outsourced its customer support and scaled 3X in just one year by focusing only on growth and marketing instead of daily firefighting.

Final Thought: The Trap That Holds You Back

"Most people spend more time working in their business than on their business." — Michael Gerber, The E-Myth.

This is a quote I read that moved me deeply and gave real meaning to my business. It made me realize that I had been working *in* my business rather than *on* it. Taking that insight, I immediately shifted my focus to working *on* my business, making it my profession.

You started your business with a vision. But right now, if you are spending most of your time fixing problems, training employees, handling escalations, and managing resignations—you are working in the business, not on it.

Breaking the Training Trap is not a choice—it is a necessity if you want to create a business that runs smoothly, grows consistently, and doesn't depend on you 24/7.

Your Next Step: Take Action Today

- **Audit your business today:** Where are you stuck? What is pulling you away from your vision?
- **Make a plan:** Identify which strategy (hiring systems, training modules, or outsourcing) fits your needs the best.
- **Take the first step:** Even a small change in the right direction will start freeing you from the trap.

It's time to take that first step. Break free from the Training Trap and unlock the path to rocket-speed growth.

Together, Stronger

You now hold a mini-Wikipedia on breaking free from the Training Trap and building a self-running, scalable business.

Now you have two choices:

- You can take all the insights and steps shared in this book as your map and walk the journey alone.
- Or, if you want me to walk alongside you, answer your queries, or guide you personally based on your specific situation, you can schedule a 1-to-1 meeting with me.

If you feel stuck anywhere or just need a little clarity to move faster, I'm just a message away.

Drop me a mail at: mayank@am2pmsupport.com

Let's work together to fast-track your business growth!